SONGS FROM
THE STYX

L.W. ROGERS & T.F. WEBB

'Songs from the Styx'
(Extended Edition)

Cover Design: DC Cover Creations

dccovercreations.com

Dedications

For my husband Andrew. Your love and
support are always there. I love you.

~ L.W.Rogers

For Mum and Dad – Your love made me.

~ T.F. Webb

Contents

Granite-grazed

Beauty

Mutiny

Birds

Curses

Whine

The Earthly Realm

Wicca

A Mother's Love

Full Moon

The Infernal Journey

By T.F. Webb

Be careful what you wish for...

Souls ripped

From battered cases

Laid to waste

In the hellhounds' wake...

And if there is a hell

Drag them there

Eternal punishment

For those things

That they deny themselves.

The Never-ending Darkness

Drifting through the hamlets

Of Anguish and Pain

Circling

Slowly

To a town called Despair

I passed through there

And the all consuming numbness

To find myself floating

In the never-ending darkness.

The Nine-Ringed Circus

Step right up!

Throw your cares away!

Buy your dream ticket

to a brighter day.

        Step right up!

      Your wish is our command.

      Live your every dream,

       come, take my hand.

Step right up!

We've all that's divine.

Live out your desires -

just sign the dotted line.

Step right up!

Take your final bow.

We've all you need

in the here and now.

Jump right in!

Take your final breath

for the one way journey

down the tunnel of eternal death...

Fleeting Creatures

We are fleeting creatures

Devil's spawn

Temporary occupants

Our bodies not our own

We are every good guy

With a wicked smile

And every bad guy

That grins at your demise.

Hell-bound

Shredded fingers

      clawing rocks,

            bleeding words

          from savage wounds.

      Spiralling

to icy depths.

     Ripped grins on angel faces,

          happily hell-bound.

Tortured souls

Nine circles

Descending

Interlinked

Never-ending

One ring

Their eternal burden

Their sins exposed

Those wicked, little tortured souls.

Slow Flow

The Styx

bewitches

its slow flow

a burning ooze

that erodes the ravaged land,

filled to over-flowing

with the dying cries

of the common man.

Thrive

This is the place where the daemons dance,

all hell let loose;

chaos at its finest.

But the Satan makes work for static hands -

No rest for the soul-less.

No sleep for the tireless.

Torture and pain the reward for the shameless,

and they'll love it every time -

Oh see how they thrive...

Granite-grazed

Ritual beating

Bare back to granite grazed

Pinned

Gasping

Frantically writhing

Skeletal plume-plucked wings discarded.

Eternally sacrificed

Permanently altered

Angels broken

by the sweetest of tortures.

Beauty

Trees bow 'neath a clotted sky

A choked sun casts no shadows

Hell whispers its sounds of fury

The wind sighs at this bleak beauty.

Mutiny

There's a child in power

wielding a shrinking shaft

His power is fading

his time slowly ending

and the battle rages on

to the music of the carrion,

the beat of bone drums

and the moans of the dying

as the fading suns look on.

There's a mutiny within

War torn wastelands

filled with passionate rebellion

The battalion of a Satan

against the minions of rival clan

where the dead will rise

and fight over who commits the better sins

in an eternal war

where neither wins.

Birds

They're different here (the birds).

A collective of introspective,

An intelligent herd,

An unkindness of ravens

With razor-sharp wit

The carrion of hell,

Deadly with sin.

A single personality

They're winged people, wild

Conspiring so loudly

As they take to the skies

They soar as they murmur

Their secrets of old

Attacking the treetops

As they drop and they roll.

See their dark, oil-slick feathers,

Obsidian eyes,

Razor-sharp beaks,

Ear-piercing cries.

Listen to their chatter

From their perch on the roof

Those paragons of wisdom

And tellers of truths.

Curses

I put my trust in you

Beneath this stormy purple sky

I await the cues

Of this never-ending ritual

Let me count the ways

That you tear at every part of me

As you build this shell

And cage me in profanity.

Whine

It's a hard addiction

Claret heats within

There's a slow constriction

Itching beneath the skin

Your maledictions

Slow-moving toxins clogging veins

Punch-drunk and listless

The tempest rages on now

It's power beautiful and deadly

My life-force turned against me

Its dying screams, the sweetest melody.

The Earthly Realm

By L. W. Rogers

Wicca

Something Wicca this way comes,

Its magick deep inside.

It fills you with its strength and power,

but this you must abide;

Harm, thee none,

Or three times back

It knows no other way.

Its magick knows no bounds,

and for this it will make you pay.

For magick is all around you,

in which you must take part.

Embrace your inner witch,

Then we can make a start.

A Mother's Love

A mother's love knows no bounds.

She'll keep away the evil hounds.

Fire, wind, water, earth

Spirit protected her from birth

Secrets held in blood and love.

Powers entangled from Heaven above.

Even in death, a mother protects

Through charms and emblems she

embeds.

There's nothing a mother wouldn't do

to protect her child through and through.

Full Moon

The full moon nears its apex

A witches coven prepares for what's next

A circle cast to harness its power

As they await the Witching Hour.

Candles lit, the fire burns

Crystals placed, the moon they yearn.

For each moon cycle, their powers

recharge

The negative energy completely purged.

They call upon their Goddess on high

For on this moon cycle, in their hearts lie

their truths and wishes laid out bare

a coven strengthening as they share.

Powers grow as the moon shines

through,

Blessing each witch to start anew.

Giving thanks to the moon on high,

Using its strength so they may thrive.

Each moon phase a witch will know

Harnessing each stage as it grows.

Until it's full, high, and proud

The full moon's power to which they bow.

Power

Ancestors of the past

Come to me and settle here

Hear my plea, I conjure thee

My time has come

So mote it be

I ask of you to bring with thee

The power of our ancestors

To flow through me

I heed your guidance, and your power

In this final witching hour.

Grant for me these few gifts

To become the vessel of eternal power

Protect the coven and through it me

I invite you in

So mote it be.

Foretold

Sinned with love

Denied a life

Offspring spawned

Forbidden delight

An act so heinous

The penalty death

For they speak

of an original sin

Death and destruction

Welcomes you in

The fire of Hell

Will force its way through

And spill on Earth

In crimson tides.

Grimoire

Leather bound, old and worn.

Intricacy of it adorns.

The fine gold edging,

of each page.

The familiar smell,

must, lavender and sage.

A book so ancient,

filled with great power.

A legacy for all witches,

its knowledge to empower.

For a Grimoire is a sacred book.

Protect it from evil,

do all that you should.

Wounded

A wound that cuts the deepest,

a scar across the heart.

It fades, but not forgotten.

For love has played its part.

Her heart now closed and cold

no trust within to hold.

Betrayal from a loved one,

It burnt her very soul.

Embers

Embers burn

In which I hold

Fierce with fury

My palm a-glow

Hidden within

It's power, strong

Extinguishes life

One spark,

You're gone.

Forsaken

Cold

Unchanging

Rage

Fury

Destruction

Obliteration

Grief

Despair

Numbness

Enduring

Vengeance

Death

For I have been forsaken.

Darkness

Tortured soul

She lies in wait

For death to claim his prize

A hue of darkness

All around

Forever tainted now.

Calling

Fire burns within me,

its gift, ever strong.

Air fills my lungs,

its essence brings life.

Water purifies my soul,

an endless stream of forgiveness.

Earth keeps me grounded,

unshaken in its form.

Spirit, although hidden,

it's a portal to the other side.

All the elements called,

I'm filled with such power.

For I am a force to be reckoned with.

This is your final hour

Burdened

The daughter of a mighty witch,

a burden it bestows.

A time will come, with in which;

she must take a hold.

Her time is near, in this she fears;

she will not be ready.

To take her rightful place as leader,

a responsibility that lays so heavy.

Her mother kind and loving,

for she feels she is not.

Something dark and twisted,

twists her into knots.

Burying it deep inside,

she smiles at the world.

A deep dark secret,

of which she knows not

Threatens to take a hold.

Dark & Light

Does darkness equate to evil

as light equates to good?

You're be born in darkness

yet live in the light,

Or born in light, yet live in sin.

There is a line that once you crossed

your fate sealed; within it you're lost.

No way of returning to the life you once knew,

A forgotten soul falling through.

Goddess

As the sunsets on this day,

we thank our Goddess, to whom we pray,

for the bountiful gifts she bestows;

her guidance, strength and love in us, it flows.

As the witching hour gets near,

we call on the elements that we hold dear.

Drawing from its almighty power,

to do our bidding in this hour.

Anthems of Angels: Part One

By L.W. Rogers

AFTERLIFE

DEATH COMES ON SWIFT WINGS,

TAKES YOU THROUGH THE CLOUDS.

TO ENTER HEAVENS MIGHTY GATES,

YOUR SOUL MUST BE PURE.

FOR SINNERS ARE NOT WELCOME HERE,

THE PITS OF HELL FACE THEM.

ONCE YOU'RE THROUGH, IT'S UP TO YOU,

YOUR AFTERLIFE IS YOURS TO MAKE.

FOR THE VERY PUREST ONES

A DIFFERENT FATE AWAITS.

YOU'LL BRANDISH WINGS OF WHITE,

SO GLORIOUS TO BEHOLD.

FOR YOU'LL BECOME AN ANGEL OF GOD,

TO PROTECT ALL THOSE BELOW

Entrance

Painful as I lie in wait,

for death to take me from this place.

Fear of going towards the unknown,

my soul I bare for all to know.

To await my judgement to be bestowed upon
me.

The reaper takes me from this place with
glee.

Is my soul pure enough for heaven's gate?

Or do the fiery pits of hell await?

Silence as I float through the ether,

towards my afterlife, it's becoming clearer.

Calmness and serenity spreads through me,

as I see the gates of my destiny.

Not of fire and brimstone as I feared.

For there is purity, warmth and love here.

The glorious gates of heaven stand tall

Its glistening lights, welcoming all.

Entry to Heaven

Heaven isn't black and white,

where you die and then ascend.

There's trials and tribulations,

even the purest must attend.

To be in God's good graces,

he needs to be absolutely sure,

that you would go to any means,

to protect the realms so pure.

To earn those feathered wings so vast,

to become a soldier for God's cause

or protector over all,

you must complete the tasks he sets.

If you pass, on to heaven you get.

Your personal clouds of white, to sit.

Duty bound, In God you trust.

Second Chances

Heaven comes in many forms,

its realms are vast and many.

For those whose path has been twisted in
life,

forever they live on clouds of white.

Their soul may not be born so pure,

but deep inside God knows more.

For God is ever knowing and true,

His decision is final, no doubt in you.

A place he'll find for you in heaven,

where your soul can be forgiven.

Fate has a way of blending the truth

Her wicked way, hidden from most

But not from God, who knows her ways

God sees through all that's blurred

And saves the souls of those that deserve.

Heaven or hell?

What if heaven isn't heaven at all?
Instead, your own personal hell.
To sit upon clouds of white,
of your past life, you dwell.

Watching as the world goes by
your loved ones as they grow.
Observing the mistakes, they make,
the evil of the world.

No voice to shout to warn them.
Nobody in which to hold.

A silence that's so deafening,

the void it burns a hole.

You yearn for just one more chance;

a chance to have your say.

To tell them how much they were loved,

you scream it every day.

Now you're just a spectator

in god's own personal war.

Is that really a heaven;

or hell in a new form?

Anthems of Angels: Part Two

By T.F. Webb

Heaven's Gates

When it ends,

when our lungs wheeze out their final
breath,

when the rot sets in -

our bodies breaking down -

when we're buried in the ground,

where will we go?

Will we roam the land,

lost souls with no home?

Haunt the ones we love or hate?

Living on the whisper of a gentle breeze

Or rattle rusty chains with the crashing
thunder,

turned away from Peter's pearly gates?

Or will they let us in

because we touched the proffered palms

with silver coated prayers

VIP passes bought and paid for

in the final aching moments

of a forced redemption?

Heaven's Rejects

In life we walk the human path.

Regrets are few.

Regrets are many.

Still we seek something beyond,

living in hope for brighter days.

Yet when our end draws close,

and we raise ourselves from sin-soaked dreams,

last minute prayers upon our lips,

hands up,

knees bent

begging for redemption

Will we face the welcome heat of Hell,

a devil's playground our protection

or suffer a purgatorial fate,

fallen from grace,

frozen,

earthbound,

in the icy blast of Heaven's cruel rejection?

Paradise

How we long to play

Amidst those frosted trees

On the silver tinted plain

Buoyed

Elated

The destination of those fated

To live in paradise

Within the comforting confines

Of ivory-towered castles in the sky.

Suits

There are more suits

than halos

in this Godforsaken town.

There are wings within the castle walls -

sergeants of a gilded king,

angels wearing frowns,

broken wings

and painted faces

from the constant beat-downs.

Bored Games

Constrained

Contained

Chessboard figures

Angels restrained

Suffocating

Pained

Pawns of a corrupt god

And his bored, twisted games.

Trinity

Three realms,

at the core the same

When the four horsemen come,

when we reach those final days,

who do we turn to?

Who do we blame?

Initium Finis

By T.F. Webb

Prophecy

Those ancient stones still quaking

Echoes and ashes turn to dust

and the battle is still raging

'tween the daemon and the
sorceress

Lust branded bone deep

Love burning to the core

Two fatal allies tussling

in a never-ending war.

Also Available

'Raising Hell' by L.W. Rogers & T.F.
Webb

Take one daemon-hating fire witch.

Add a haemophobic daemon with a near
impossible task.

Sprinkle in some dark magic

and watch the world burn!

An excerpt from 'Raising Hell':

Chapter 1

Cadence

I gasp as I wake, sweat pouring off me. My heart is racing at an unnatural speed. It takes me a while to focus and realise what is happening. That all too familiar feeling of burning up like I was still in my dream, the realisation that the sight before me is literal, seeing my not-so-clean sheets as they become engulfed in flames. I calm my thoughts, close my eyes, raise my hands, palms down, over my flaming duvet and I cast until the fire is out and I begin to cool off. I climb out of bed and grab the now very charred duvet in my arms, then throw it into a rubbish bag. *Thank god I didn't burn the apartment down.*

I look at my clock. 09:02. *'Crap! I'm late for work.'* I quickly shower, scrubbing away any stench of smoke or charred flesh from my body. I climb out, patting myself dry. I can see the wounds are already healing. By the time I get to work they won't even be noticeable. Perks of being a witch; fast healing. I throw my hair up in a wet bun and dress as quick as I can. I have no time to preen this morning.

I call down to Tobias telling him to bring the car to the front and grab my bag, phone and folder as I head for the elevator. Tobias is out front, already holding the passenger door open for me as I exit the apartment complex.

"Ma'am." His head lowers in a respectful gesture as I slide into my seat. He closes the door, heading around to the driver's side and starts the car. We drive into the centre of town with minimal interruptions from traffic...thank god! I have no patience for that shit, especially when I'm already late.

As we park in the basement of the building my phone rings. I rummage for it amongst the crap that is housed in my bag. *I seriously need to de-clutter.* It stops ringing before I have chance to answer, which leaves me cursing under my breath. Tobias opens the door, offering his hand. I take it and step from the car, only to be accosted by the head of my security team.

"Miss Winters, we have a situation," Trevor informs me, his expression firm and serious.

"What now, Trevor?" I ask sternly, not impressed that I haven't even been greeted with even a sniff of my morning latte.

"Sorry Ma'am, but it's extremely urgent."

I sigh. "Well get on with it," I snap as I

walk to the elevator, Trevor by my side. "We've had a break in. Your office..." There is hesitation in his voice. I turn to him, face hard, cold. I say nothing as we enter the lift. I press for the top floor and the door closes.

"Has anything been taken?" I ask as the lift ascends, trying to comprehend how this could have happened.

"Not that we can see, the team are doing a full sweep of the building. We also have a team on their way to check the security, and IT to ensure we haven't been hacked."

I say nothing, processing what I've been told and wondering how this could happen. I have the highest spec, up-to-date security system there is, on top of security spells which are cast when I leave the building. Whoever this was it wasn't a 'human' intrusion. That I can say with absolute certainty. However, I'm dumbfounded as to why it's happened or who it could be. I don't think it's personal. My private life is very separate from business; well, to an extent.

I have supernaturals working for me, but that's only because I have to. My mother always says it is a means to an end and a way to keep track of the supernatural world. Daemons (full and half breeds), witches, warlocks, wolves; you name it, I have it. I have a variety of supernaturals on my payroll for whatever needs that may arise. All come with their own expertise. You may have guessed what wolves and daemons are used for... muscle, pure and simple. Daemons aren't the smartest of the bunch but they have their uses, and wolves, well need I say more?

My company (or should I say my mother's company) deals with rare antiquities. They're not your usual rare antiquities. Well we do get the odd one, but on the whole, we deal with ones with supernatural origins. We keep a log of all the antiquities we now have and the ones we previously had and where they are in the world. Yes, we do sell them, after all we are a business, but we vet the buyers and we have a tracking spell on everything we sell. If they sell it on, without prior permission, their punishment is severe.

Yes, I may sound harsh and you probably think I'm being a bitch but growing up in the supernatural world makes you grow up very quickly and you learn to trust no one. I'm the boss. I can't be seen to have a weak spot. When my mother passes over, the company will be mine, as will her place as coven leader. No pressure!

I have to be strong for my family and the business. I have responsibilities and with them comes the hard truth that I have to be ruthless, especially in a world run by men. No man is ever going to get between me and my goals. Over my cold, dead body! Hell would have to freeze over before I let a man tell me what to do.

As the lift comes to a stop, the doors open and the hustle and bustle from the 'break-in' is apparent. The large reception area is crammed with staff and security, who are combing every inch of the place for any evidence that the intruder may have left behind. The search will be in vain. If 'someone' (I say that loosely, as I'm almost certain it's a supernatural) has managed to gain access to the building, then they are smart enough to not leave any clues.

Trevor continues to follow as I enter my office at the far end of the corridor. As the door closes behind me, I can sense that I'm not alone. I chuck my belongings on my desk, taking a breath. Gritting my teeth in frustration, I turn to see Trevor standing guard inside the office. He's very formal...hands crossed behind his back, his stance that of a true bodyguard, head facing forward. Not even eye contact.

"Is there anything else?" I probe him further as I lean onto my desk in a slightly relaxed manner which just feels so unnatural for me.

"No Ma'am. I just think it's important that security is increased until the suspect is apprehended." His face never falters, nor moves its position.

Like a jolt, I'm out of my 'semi-relaxed' pose and walking a few feet towards him, feeling a little ticked off that he would take it upon himself to make this decision. Yes, he maybe Head of Security but everything, and I mean everything, goes through me. No questions asked.

"Do you not think I can take care of myself, Trevor?" I ask, moving closer to him, hand raised, palm up. I look at my hand and a small flame appears. Trevor's eyes now move from the fixed gaze to the flame that is building within the palm of my hand.

"No Ma'am," he says quickly with a nervous quiver in his voice.

"Well then…" I close my hand, extinguishing the fire. I head to my desk. "Don't assume I need more security. I can handle myself, as you well know. As for security, I agree it needs to be increased. Especially at night. Please see to that and leave me to my day."

"Yes Ma'am." The door goes once more and I'm finally left in peace. I walk around to my desk, removing the crap I'd flung on it. I take a seat and grab the pile of mail staring at me. *'Ugh! I hate paperwork.'*

"Julie…" I buzz my receptionist, "Could I get a large Latte, extra sugar." I click off before she even has time to acknowledge the request. I am in need of some serious caffeine if I am going to get through today.

Before settling into the tasks for the day, there's one call I should make. After all, it is her business, so she should know what has happened. I dial and before it even gets to the second ring, she answers.

"Everything okay, Cadence? It's an unusual time for you to call." My mother was always very perceptive; one of her many qualities. But I suppose being an empath gives her a heads up in all situations.

"Hi mum. I just wanted to let you know what's happened here," I begin to tell her. I fill her in on the morning's issues. She listens intently, not interrupting me until she knows I have said what I need to. She seems un-bothered about the break in but says she will speak to the coven about it. There is a long pause before the silence is broken.

"What else?" she asks. I can feel my brow crease in confusion. I've told her everything to date.

"That's it. Once I know more, I'll let you know. You know I will."

"Did anything happen at home?" she

asks. You can't get anything past an empath, especially when she is your mother.

I roll my eyes and proceed to tell her about my slight mishap with the bedding and my dream. She doesn't seem too concerned, which she shouldn't. It's not the first time this has happened and I'm sure it won't be the last. True, it's becoming more of a regular occurrence, but I can handle it. I think my hormones are just playing up.

"Have you started preparing for your rite, Cadence?" she asks softly. I roll my eyes again.

"Not yet mum, but I will. I have plenty of time."

"Not that much time, Cadence. It's important. You can't become coven leader until you have completed this. I know you're extremely busy. How about I gather the ingredients for you? Good, then that's settled. You need to get the grimoire for it and start researching. I'll call you tonight, okay? Love you." Before I can even protest, she hangs up.

I slump back in my chair. My head is beginning to throb from all the stress. I know she means well and wants the best for me, but I know once I do what she asks of me that it will affect her and her powers and I just don't think I'm ready. I'm not ready for her to leave me.

I close my eyes for a brief period, head whirling with ideas of how to get out of it. I hear a gentle knock on the door and Julie enters with my drink. She places it on the desk quietly and leaves. I crack one eye open once I hear the door click shut to check if she has left. I sigh and grab the hot drink from my desk. Caffeine; my best friend. I take my time with it, knowing once it is gone I'll have to start today's tasks.

I flit through my diary, checking what I

have on today. I am relieved to note I have no meetings scheduled. I don't have the social skills to suck up to prospective clients on a good day let alone today. I sift through the mail stacked on my desk. Most of it is twaddle, so I throw it in the recycling. A nagging feeling gnaws at me. I am annoyed...more than annoyed. I am pissed. Pissed that someone could not only bypass my state of the art security, but also my high-powered security spells. I can feel my frustration and anger begin to bubble to the surface. My hands begin to steam. I have to calm down or I'll set fire to the office.

I walk over to the sink in the right corner of the office, turning the cold tap on and running my wrists and hands under it. I close my eyes as I will myself to calm down. If you haven't guessed, I have active powers as a witch. They are deeply connected to my emotions, which is never good, especially for a female. Invoking fire is my dominant power and it's the one that gets me in more trouble than I'd care to admit.

Once calm and collected I decide to delve into this mysterious security breach and see if there was anything missing. I decide to visit the antiquities library we have a couple levels down and review things from there. I tell Julie to forward any calls relating to the breach to my mobile. Anything else can wait. She nods in acknowledgement. I take to the stairs, not having the patience to wait for elevators.

The antiquities library is busier than usual. I head to the secure cabinet which stores the paper inventory of what we have in the library alongside separate folders for ones that have been sold and pending to come in. I insist on paper copies and electronic copies for situations just like the one presenting itself today. If we have been hacked, there's no certainty that they couldn't have been altered. I start with the relics we physically have with us. Everything is listed alphabetically and the location of each item is clearly documented. All I have to do is go through them.

"We've already gone through the inventory lists, Miss Winters," I hear an unfamiliar male voice tell me. I turn to find who it is and find a young man in a grey suit and glasses standing a few feet from me. He holds his hand out for me to shake, which in turn makes me fold my arms, annoyed.

"I'm sorry Miss Winters, I didn't mean any offence. I didn't want you wasting your time on something we had already thoroughly checked."

"I'm sure you have thoroughly checked, but for my own peace of mind I want to go through them myself. Have the electronic files been checked?" I ask. He nods.

"We haven't found anything missing."

"Hmmm." I turn and walk away, continuing with my checks. As I near the end I reach the same conclusion. Nothing is missing. I peruse the pending folder; Nothing. I start sifting through the sold folder; again nothing. I take the folders back to my office to check against the electronic files. It is mundane and boring and yes, I know they checked them all, but I need to see it for myself.

I keep flicking between folder and computer comparing the two, then automatically pressing enter for each item. I continue until I accidentally press enter before checking the file. I back up, look at the item on the screen and what was in the folder, and do a double take. There is an item missing from the electronic file that is still in the paper file. Odd. I look at the item in question on the electronic file compared to the paper file. It is held within the sold files, which is very strange. It wasn't of particular interest, just your bog standard athame, of no known origin. It wasn't heavily magical from the assessments. It was sold almost fifteen years ago, so before my time. I take a picture of it with my phone and make a mental note to ask my mother about it.

I call Trevor in and ask him to return the files to the antiquities library, emphasising that it needs to be securely locked as soon as he's there. Opening my laptop once again, I enter the details I have on the athame into Google. I scroll through pages of athames with similar descriptions but come up empty. If it's important surely there would be some evidence somewhere? I decide to contact the buyer to discuss it further with her. The voicemail clicks in so I leave a message. The buyer is only a couple hours away. I could go in person in the hope of catching her at home, but do I really want to waste the rest of my day doing, what could be, a waste of my time? No.

I continue the day as best I can. I take leave early and decide to pay my mother a visit. I will discuss the athame further when I see her.

Coming Soon...

'Earthbound (Raising Hell: Book Two)'

By L.W.Rogers & T.F.Webb

Two warring Satans.

One angry witch.

A wrecked daemon.

The apocalypse.

An Excerpt from 'Earthbound':

Prologue

Blaine

I'm flying. Not like the fun kind of flying where you have wings and soar and dip on gusting thermals and look down upon a Lilliputian world. Not the kind of flying where your heart is elevated and everything takes your breath away and you feel so happy and unafraid that you don't think about the very definite possibility that you could possibly be an angel, or a bird, or maybe even something as mechanical as a plane.

The kind of flying that I am talking about is that long, drawn out kind that comes after you fall but you've yet to hit the ground at the end. The moment that comes after you have pitched yourself absolutely recklessly from the edge of a cliff and rock bottom is so far from your thoughts that maybe you aren't even flying. Maybe you are floating. Time is suspended and your consciousness has travelled to another plane for what is probably only the 20 or so seconds it would actually take to hurtle to your inevitable brutal, bloody death.

Except now I AM hurtling. I'm falling so fast that the ground is no longer surrounded by trees and rocks and the greenest grass I have ever seen. No; the floor is not a welcoming carpet of emerald fuzz, but a blackened slab of crispy seaweed graffiti. And I know it's going to hurt like a bitch when I hit.

Except it doesn't.

Instead, I feel nothing.

I hear nothing.

I see nothing.

I am nothing.

Chapter One

Blaine

I think I'm dying.

That can't be right. Daemons don't die. Yet, here I am staring through a black mist into reddened skies, but this is not Hell, just a first-rate rip off of its crimson palette.

This sky is filled with plumes of smoke and falling flame. I can hear the pained shrieks nearby. This world is dying and there is nothing I can do to save it.

I'd like to say it's not my fault, but somehow I think it may be. It usually is. The carnage that lies around me can only be a consequence of my previous actions. I just can't figure out how.

I look around and realise that there is no sign of Cadence. There's plenty of smouldering heath-land, and in the distance, I can see the shattered shell of a town. The air is filled with the moans of the fading. My nostrils fill with the acrid smell of burning and decay.

When I first awoke I thought I was back home. Sadly, I am not. Instead, I find myself in a new kind of hell.

My contact on the earthly plane was murdered by my brethren. I needed to find a new contact, and my celestial counterpart Lailah went to find one. The person she found was a long shot at best. A man-hating, daemon-hating witch, from the beginning, Cadence showed resistance to the idea of having any involvement at all (probably due to the fact that I am a male daemon). Lailah persisted, but seemingly to no avail. Then things became even more messed up when Lailah was discovered creeping around the outskirts of the infernal realm. The Satan decided to torture her to find out who the mole was that was doling out Hell's secret information (if you haven't guessed already, that would be me). I was forced to leave my home as the chance of discovery at this point was way too high. I visited a satanic witch, obtained a body forged by magick, then decided to approach Cadence myself. Things didn't go to plan. One thing led to another, the proverbial shit hit the fan and before you could say 'World's end' the apocalypse happened.

Now here I am; just another daemon coasting around in a man-shaped taxi. At least, I should be, but something seems to have gone horribly wrong. My rather attractive body is now mangled, and warped. I've tried to escape, but for some unknown reason I am now caged within the confines of this useless shell. Not only that, I can feel burning, searing pain ripping through every nerve ending, every muscle, and all across the skin. I shouldn't be able to feel it. Not at all. As a daemon, I should be so wonderfully detached from it all. But for some reason I can feel every last twitch, itch, ache and burn. The brain within this body has decided to stop cooperating.

I'm starting to wonder if part of this problem is to do with the body that I have been so generously 'gifted'. It's strange that everything seems to have happened since the ritual was completed. I've never had a body 'made' for me before, but ever since the spell was cast I have been feeling more than a little out of sorts.

The majority of my kinsmen revel in the thrill of possession, but I'm not the kind of daemon that enjoys taking over someone else's body. It's never been my thing, hence why I approached Valeria in the first place. I could have the vessel to travel the human world, and not have to violate a living person to do so. I know, who'd have thought a child of Hell would care, right?

For me, it was more about the discomfort level of knowing that somewhere in that body would be the soul of whoever had been possessed. There is always a risk that said soul could fight back. There was always the absolute certainty that someone would contact the church and an exorcism would take place. That in itself, although inconvenient, wasn't a problem. If a daemon is exorcised it's merely expelled from the body it has acquired, therefore it tends to either return to Hell or move along to the next vulnerable individual to cross their path. It is simple enough for one of us to remove ourselves from these mobile tombs anyway. Well, until now.

It must be the magic. It has to be.

Another searing pain rips through my limbs, causing my body to contort in a wholly inhuman manner. Muscles spasm and tendons strain. If I didn't know any better I'd think that this carcass was trying to reject me. The aroma of burnt flesh tells me that its days may be numbered anyway. But I do know better, because ever since I found myself lying here on this desolate plain I have been trying to shrug off this clinging corpse. It could merely be that I am in a weakened state, a symptom of being at the centre of a world changing event. However, my mind keeps straying back to that damned spell. If I ever get this situation sorted I will hunt Valeria down and demand some answers. Or forcibly obtain them. I don't care. Either way I will find out what the hell is going on.

It would be fair to say that I've never been as confused as I am right now, because what I am experiencing in this moment doesn't feel like a rejection. Rather, it feels like the kind of hug that an obsessed fan would give their idol. The kind where it feels as though ribs will be cracked and they won't ever let you go. But that can't be.

The errant thought is horrific, but I cannot dismiss the possibility out of hand. If this body is embracing my being, then there is every chance that it could fuse to me. I would be stuck inside, forever in a state of symbiosis. If that happened, I could lose myself. I would have to live in a constant state of fear that this body will take over the essence of me. I would be possessed by my body. The irony is not lost on me. The idea makes me shudder which causes another round of shooting pains to fire through every nerve ending. I fight against the blackness taking me, seethe and spasm to the inferno in my veins, then wane under the weight of the slow descending obsidian mist. Then there is nothing.

Coming Soon...

'Cadence' (A Raising Hell Novella)

By L.W. Rogers

Raised by witches.

A talent for fire.

New powers can be a real bitch.

Coming Soon...

'Lailah' (A Raising Hell Novella)

By T.F. Webb

Captured.

Incarcerated.

Wingless.

It turns out Hell is far worse than it sounds.

Acknowledgements

I would like to thank my parents and husband Andrew who have all supported me so much in this journey as a writer and have never doubted me.

I would also like to say a huge thank you to my friend and co-writer of this book, T. F Webb. It has been an amazing, fun process and I look forward to our future work together.

~ L.W. Rogers

Thank you to my family for the people you are, the belief that you have, and the person you help me to strive to be. For my children – you're not going to have to knock for a little while at least. I love you all without limits.

Massive hugs for my co-writer and friend. Mrs Rogers, it's been a pleasure, an experience, and the most fun I've had in a long time. I can't wait to do it all again.

Thank you those who came and stayed on this long, long journey. Thank you to those who came and left. All of you have left me with some of the best lessons, and have helped me in so many ways. You are all appreciated so much more than I could ever put into words.

~ T.F.Webb

We would both like to show massive appreciation for our cover designer, David Collins, and our cover animator, Morgan Wright.

Lastly, we would like to give a huge thank you to our editors and beta readers for doing an amazing job. Thanks guys. We appreciate you and all of your hard work.

~ L.W. Rogers & T.F.Webb

About the Author

L.W. Rogers

Laura Rogers is a writer, poet and co-author of 'Songs from the Styx' and 'Raising Hell'. This is her first published book and she has several other works in progress. Her passion is writing for the supernatural, fantasy genre, her favourite being the vampire niche.

Laura is a mother of four, midwife and beautician, but that doesn't stop her from finding the time to write when she can, along with adding writing courses to her portfolio. It has been her passion since the age of 8 to become a published author and she has worked towards her goal through her life.

She has undertaken several writing courses online to build on her skills as a writer and is looking forward to commencing her Masters in Creative Writing in the fall.

You can find Laura online at:

Twitter: twitter.com/ilvsupernatural

WordPress: ilvsupernatural.wordpress.com

About the Author

T.F. Webb

T.F. Webb is a writer, poet, and co-author of 'Songs from the Styx' and 'Raising Hell'. An avid reader of fiction and poetry, she has a Bachelor of Arts (Hons) degree in English Literature. She is currently studying for her MA in Creative Writing.

T.F.Webb works out of her home on the edge of Dartmoor National Park in the South West of England. Her writing room is her sanctuary, where she surrounds herself with the genres she loves the most. If she's not writing she can be found reading horror, fantasy, or paranormal books or watching films from the same genres. When she is not immersing herself in fiction, she can be found taking long walks with her family, looking after her children and fur babies, or trying to blend in with her surroundings.

You can find T.F. Webb online at:

Twitter: twitter.com/tf_webb

Facebook: facebook.com/TFWebbwrites

Instagram: instagram.com/t.f.webb9

Wordpress: www.tfwebb.com

Printed in Great Britain
by Amazon

22656798R00076